ALL ABOUT THE BODY

ANATOMY AND PHYSIOLOGY

Speedy Publishing LLC
40 E. Main St. #1156
Newark, DE 19711
www.speedypublishing.com
Copyright 2016

All Rights reserved. No part of this book may be reproduced or used in any way or form or by any means whether electronic or mechanical, this means that you cannot record or photocopy any material ideas or tips that are provided in this book

Do you know what the parts of your body are and how they function?

The study of the human body's shape and form is called **Anatomy**.

Let's review the parts of the body from top to bottom. We have the head, neck, two arms, torso, and the two legs.

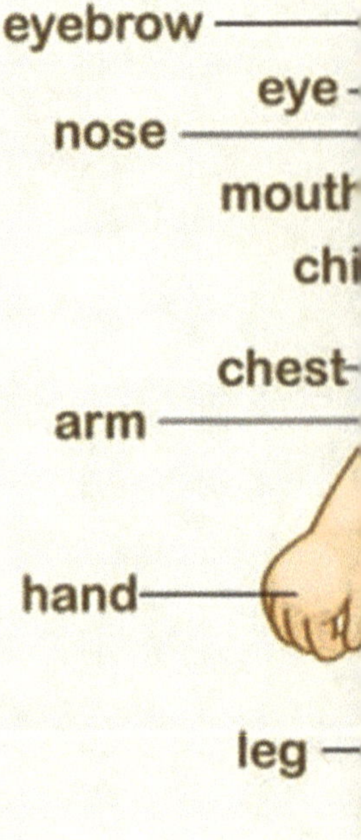

MY BODY

forehead
ear
cheek
tooth
tongue
lip
stomach
knee
foot
hair
head
neck
shoulder
back
elbow
waist
bottom
finger
ankle
heel

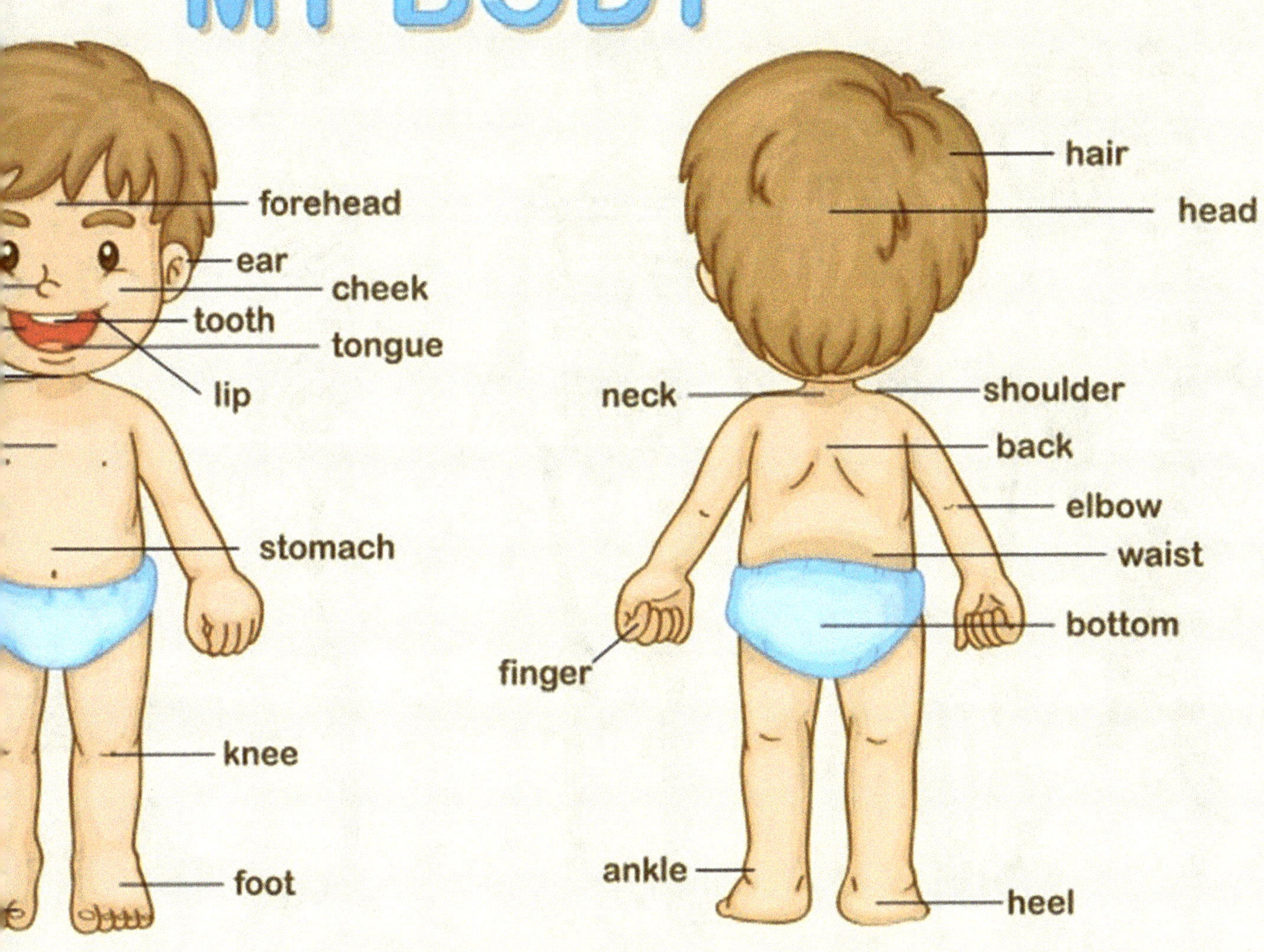

Skeleton

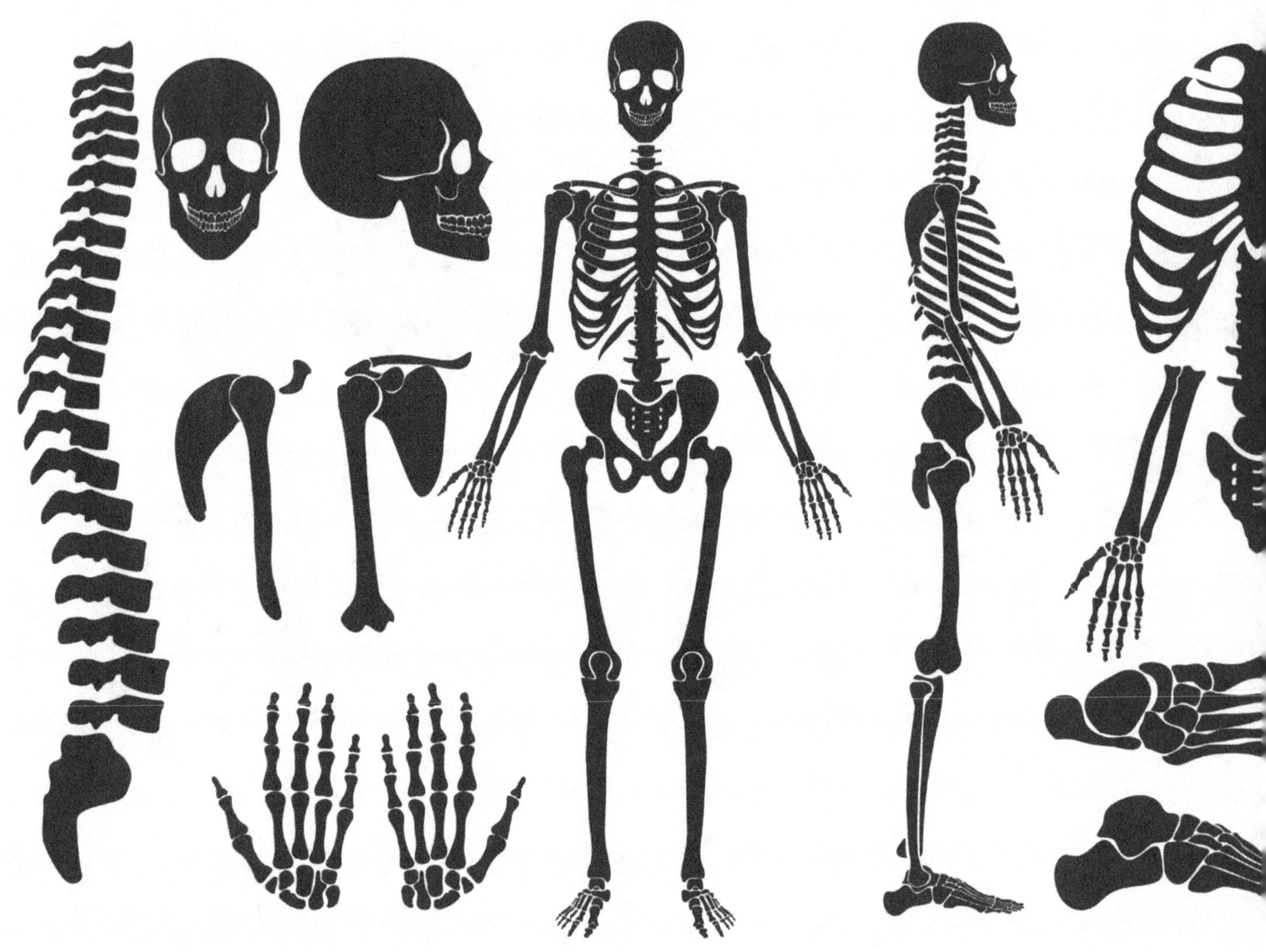

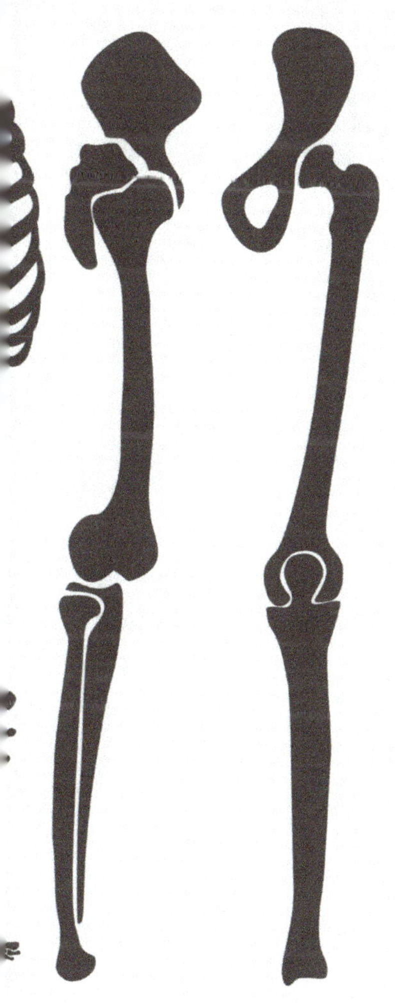

A **strong skeleton** made of bone and cartilage determines the body's shape. At the back of the skeleton is the **spine**, which contains the vertebral column that surrounds the spinal cord.

The **spinal chord** is composed of nerves that connect the brain to the rest of the body. This is where the signals pass from the body to the brain, and from the brain to the rest of the body.

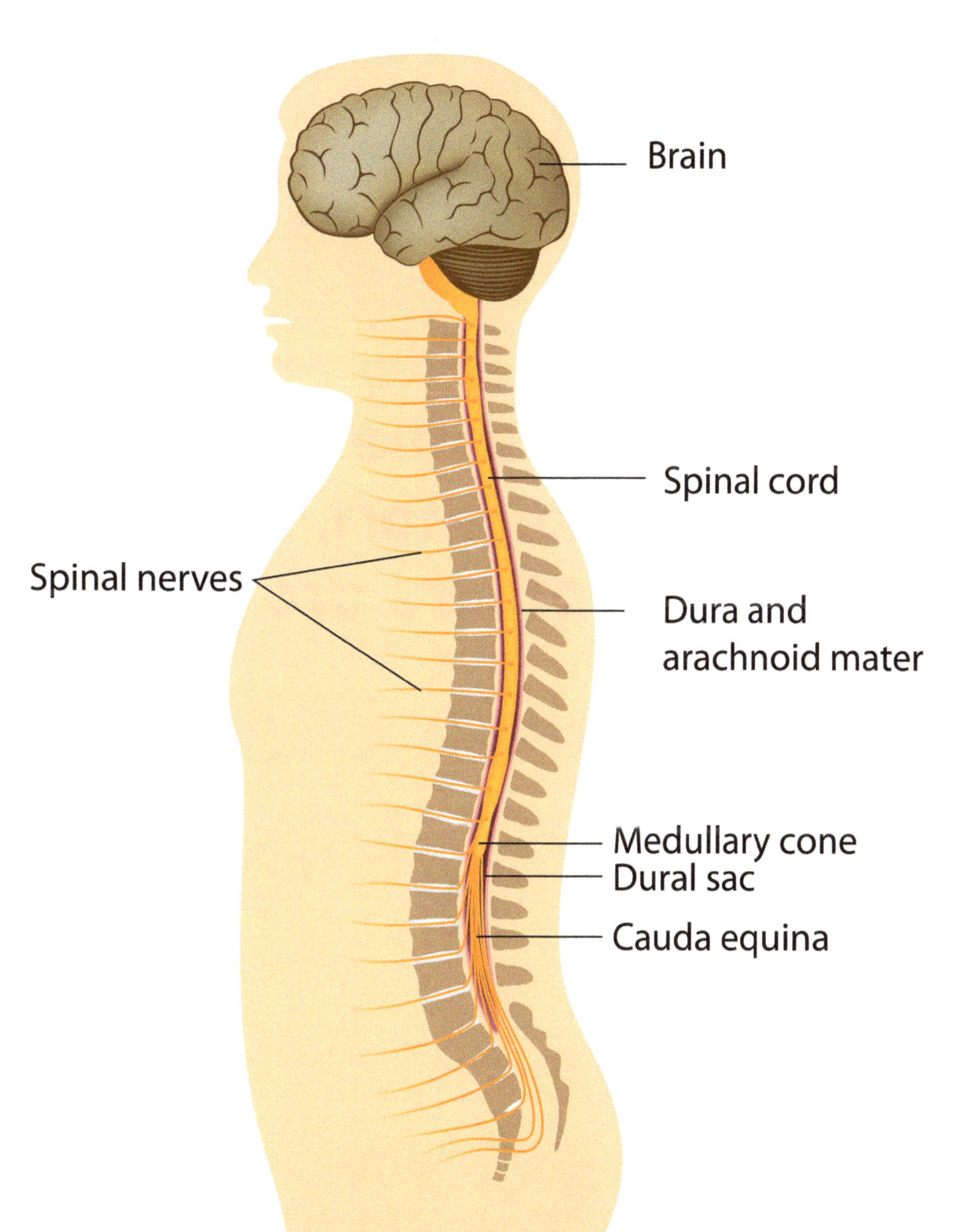
Brain
Spinal cord
Spinal nerves
Dura and
arachnoid mater
Medullary cone
Dural sac
Cauda equina

Why is it that some people are tall, some are short, some are fat, and others are thin?

These differences are influenced by the shape of the skeleton and the distribution of muscles and fatty tissue. These vary greatly with age and gender, and what you inherit from your parents. There is no one “right” body type.

Human Body Systems

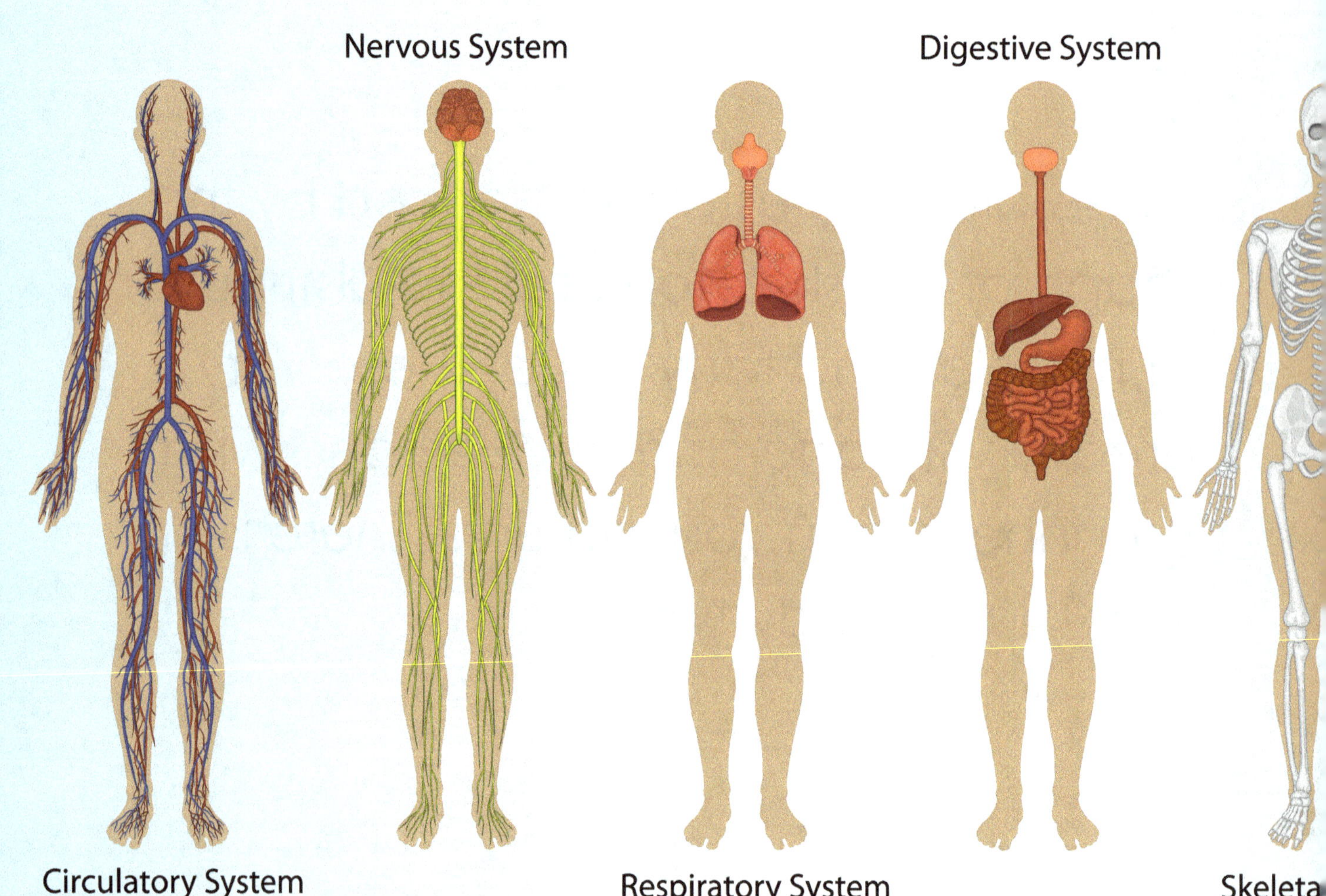

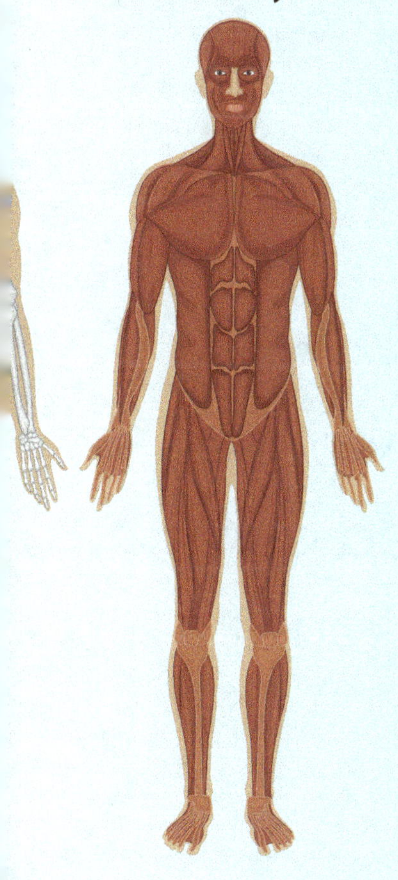
Muscular System

m

Now that we know the main parts of the body, let's see how they function. The study of how the human body functions is called **Physiology**. The body is composed of many systems of organs that help the body work.

Let's discuss what these are.

What is the nervous system?

This the central command. The brain sends messages to the other body parts through the nerves and specialized cells called neurons, and gets information back the same way.

There is a central nervous system, like a highway for messages, and the peripheral nervous system that connects to every part of the body. The brain and the spinal cord play important roles in directing the body.

The **brain** is the center of our thoughts, it interprets what our body senses from our environment and reports through the nervous system, and it controls how we react.

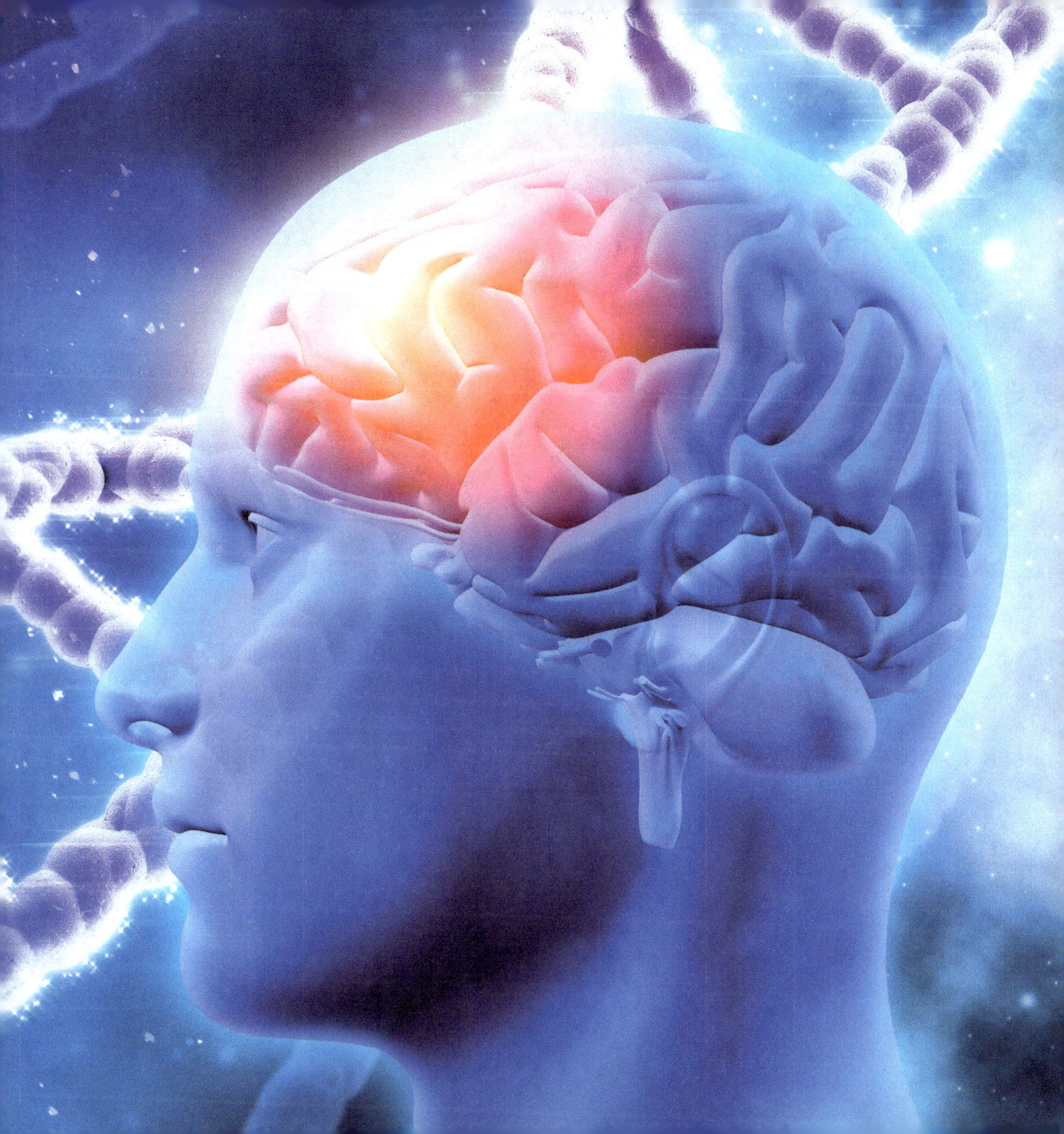

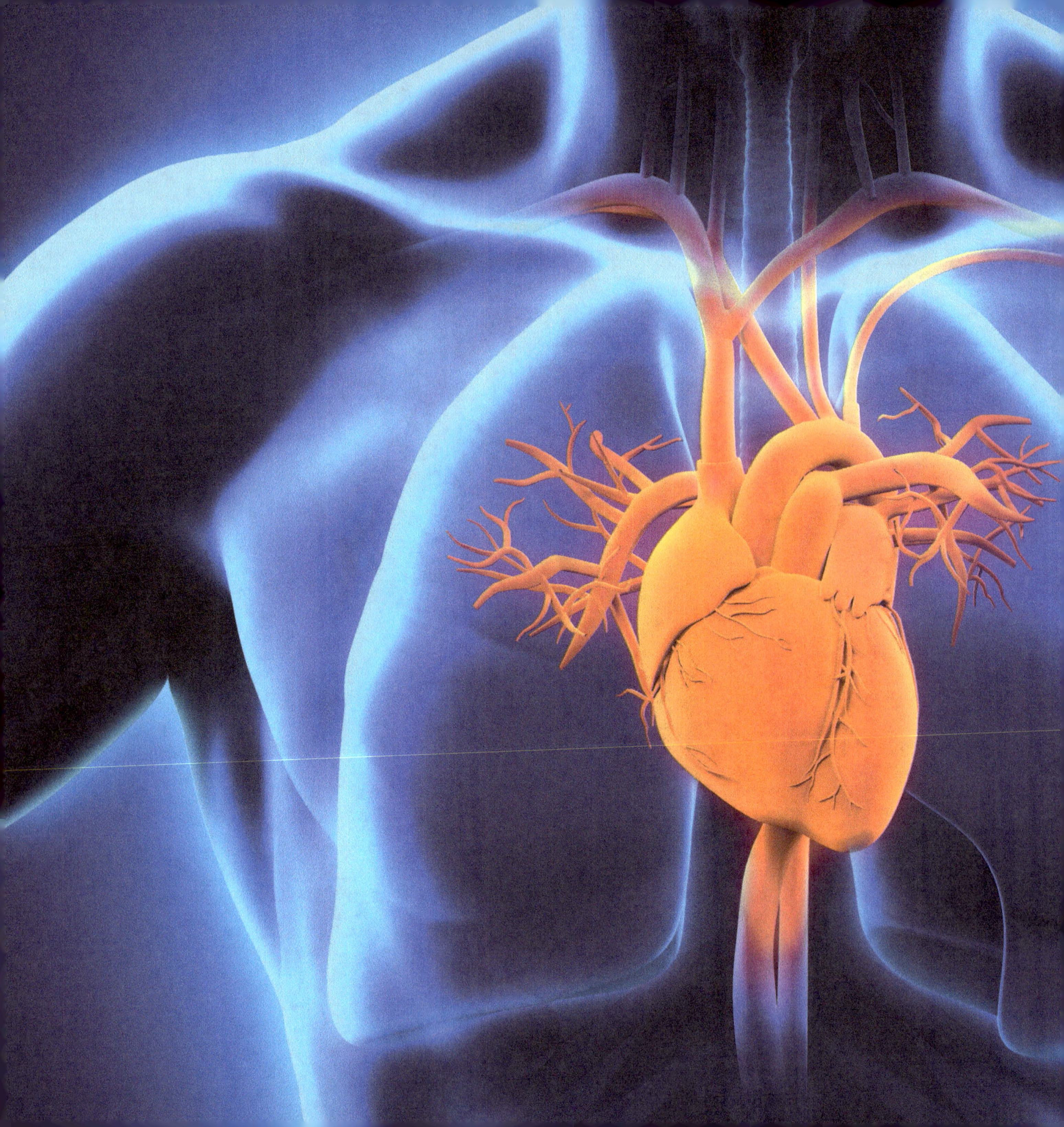

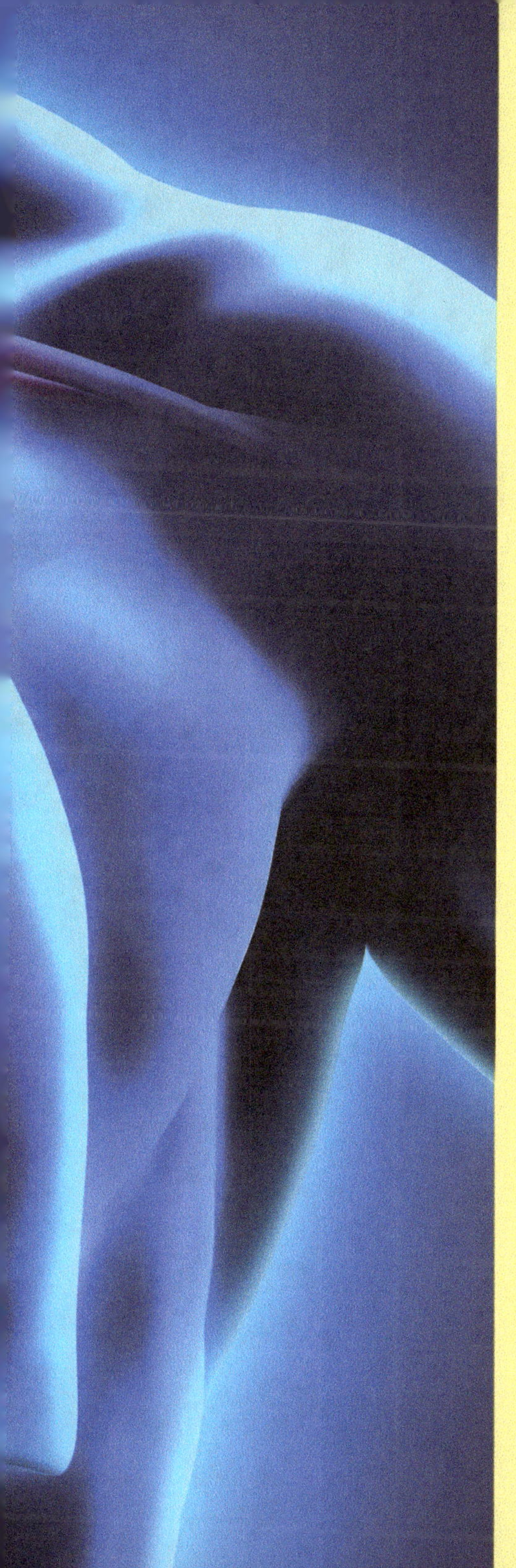

What is the cardiovascular system?

Its main organ is the **heart**, which pumps blood to supply oxygen to the different parts of the body through the blood vessels. The heart is as big as your fist and is located inside your rib cage on the left side.

What is the respiratory system?

It is responsible for our breathing. The main organs here are the **lungs**. We take in air through our nose and mouth, and the air goes through the trachea and then to the lungs, where the oxygen leaves the air to get carried to every cell in our body.

Carbon dioxide and other gases that are not needed by our body move from our blood into our lungs, and we breathe them out to get rid of them.

What is the digestive system?

It is the system that converts the food we eat into the energy we need to move our body parts and to think. Food passes though the digestive tract, composed of the mouth, esophagus, stomach, and intestines, and is then excreted.

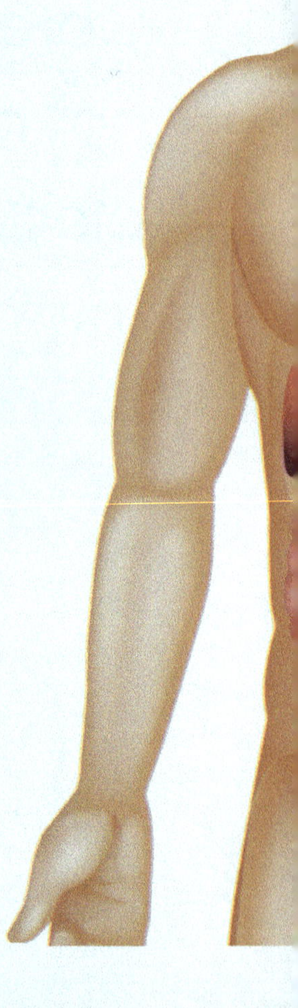

an Digestive System (Male & Female)

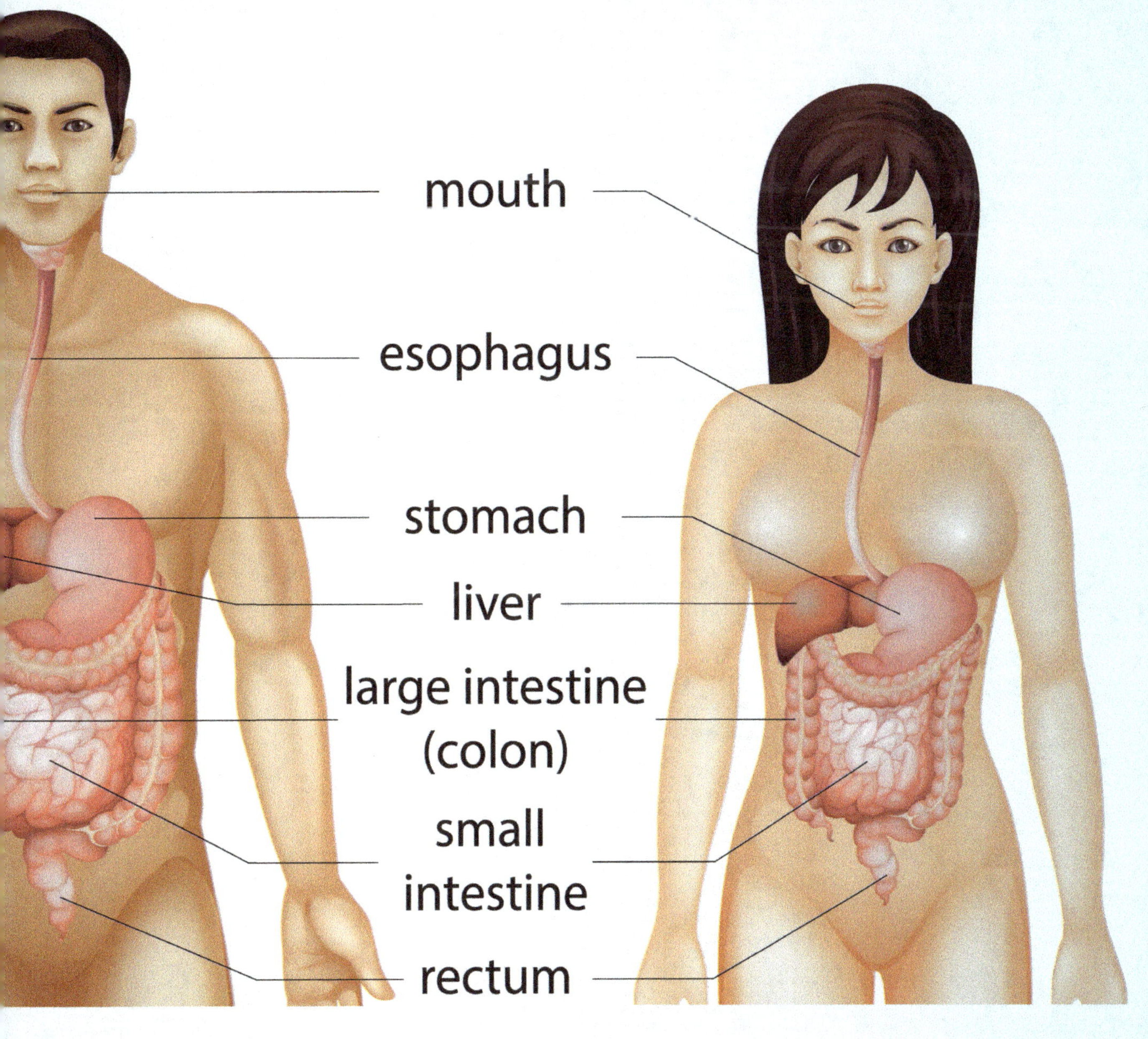

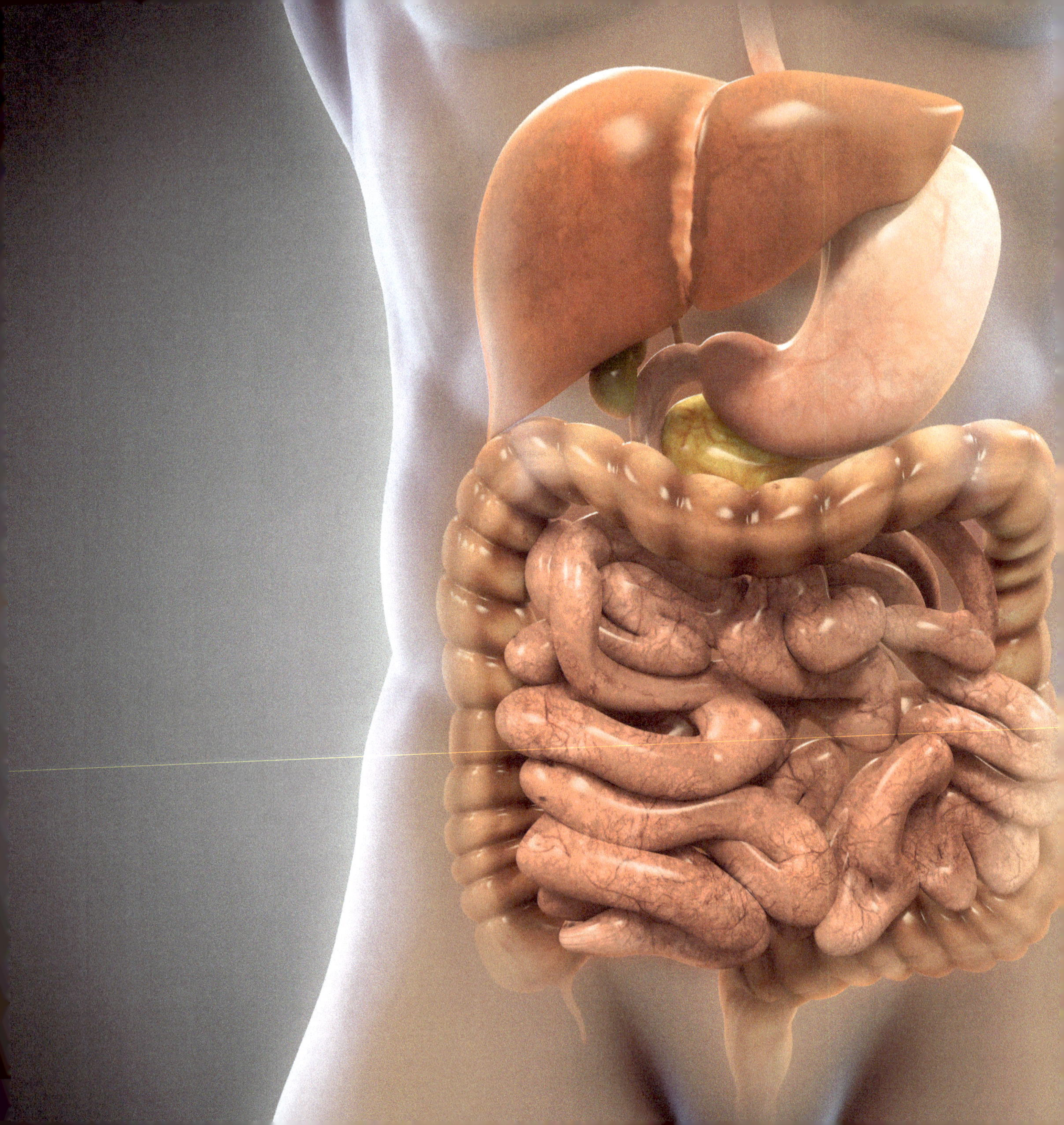

The organs that help the stomach and intestines digest the food are the pancreas, liver, and gall bladder. These organs supply the hormones necessary to break down the food and turn it into energy.

What is the urinary system?

It makes sure your body gets rid of waste and excess fluids. The fluids go through the kidneys, where they are filtered and cleaned.

HUMAN URINARY SYSTEM

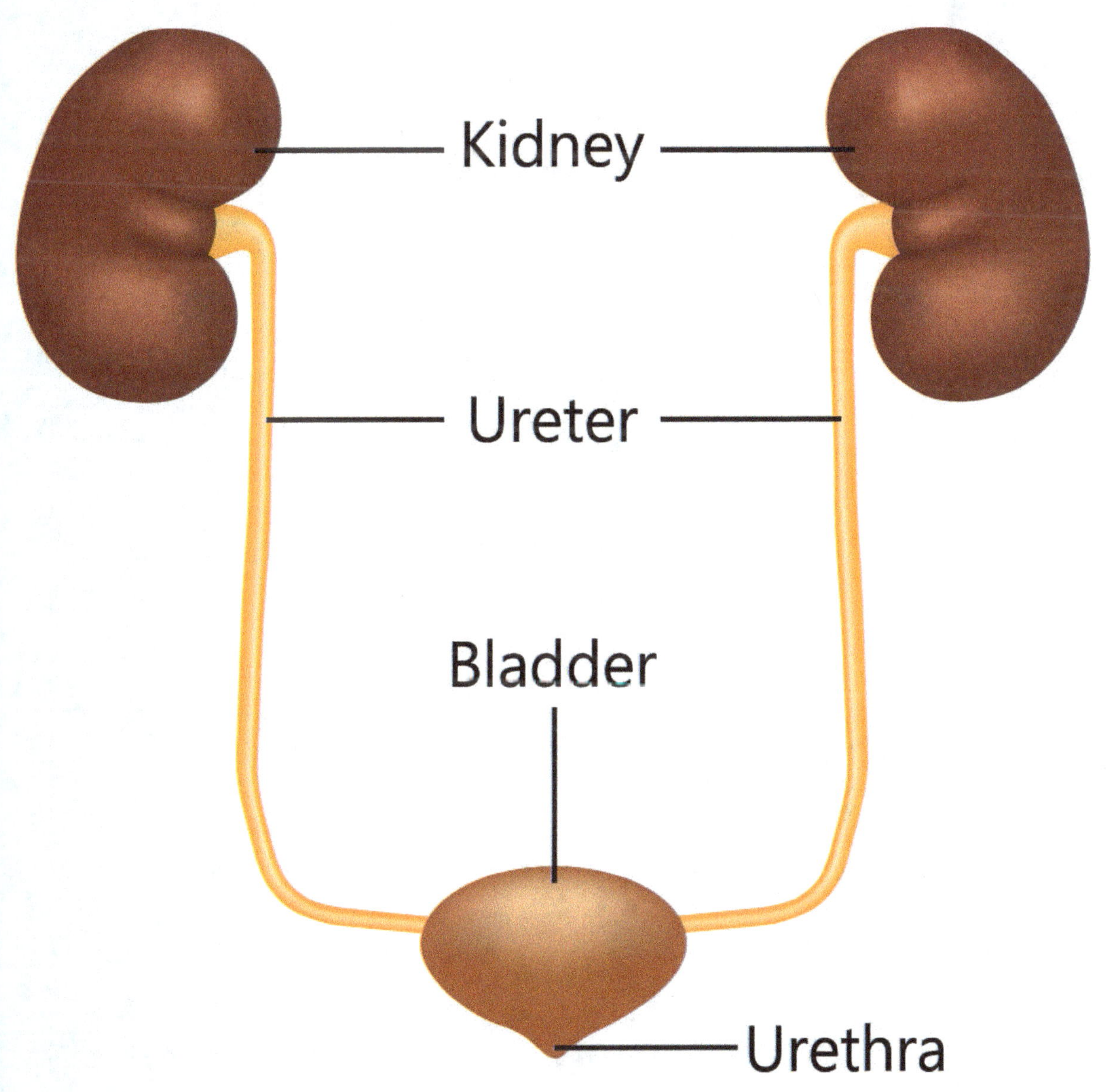

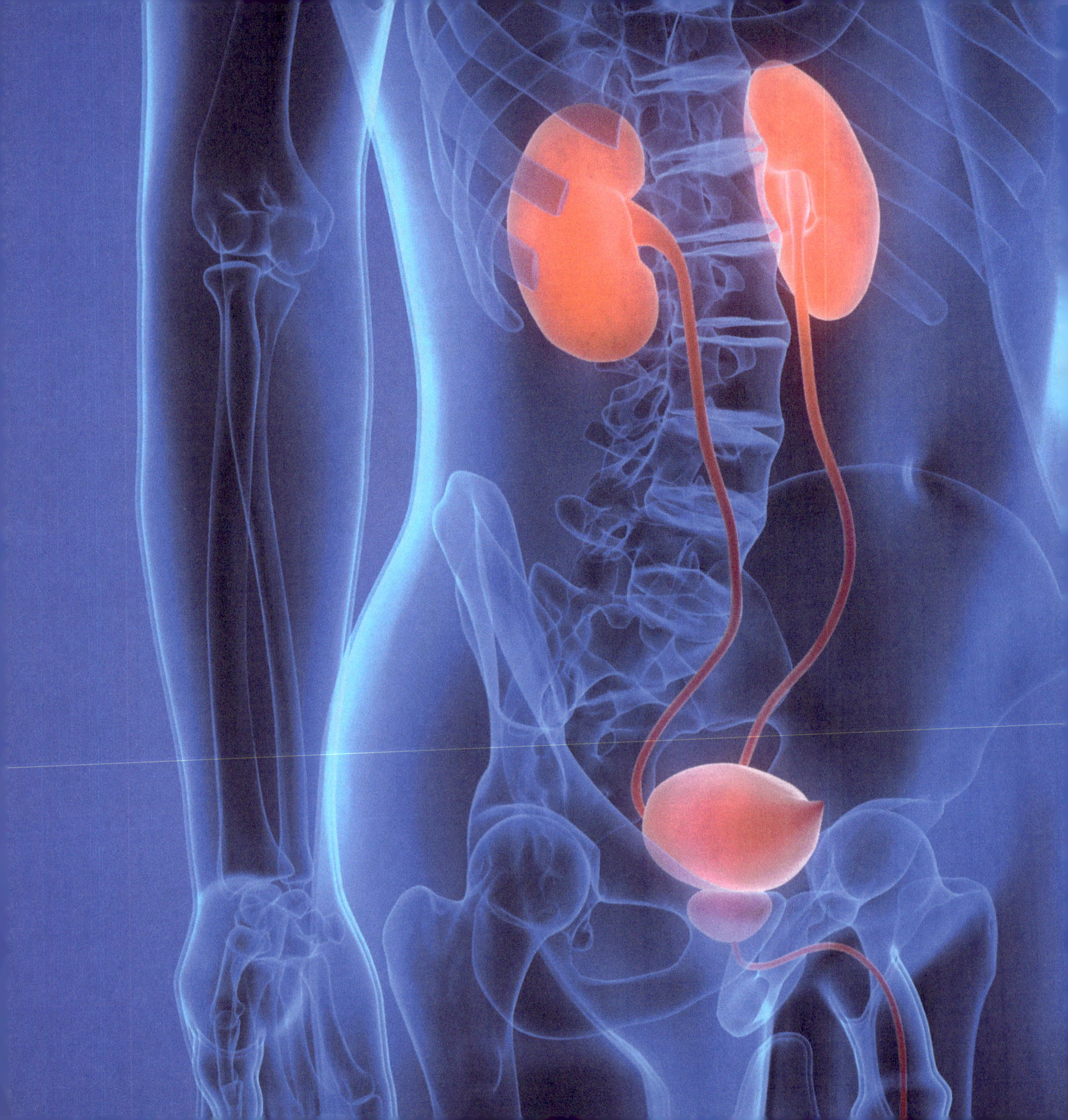

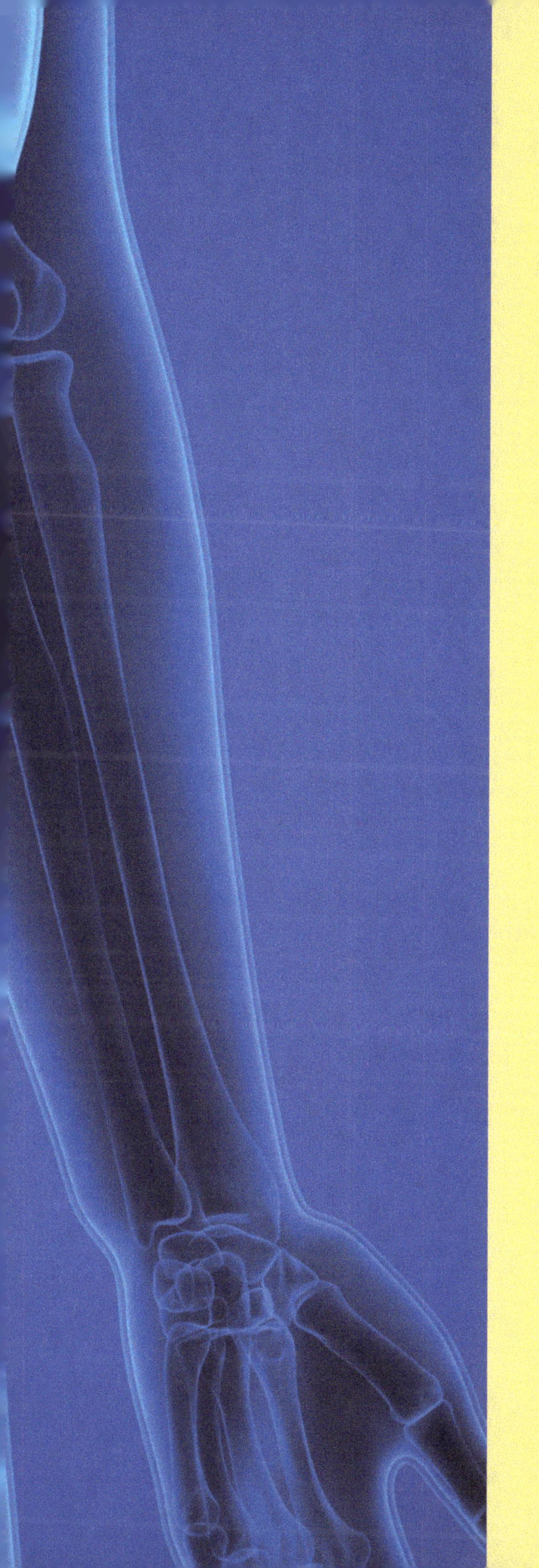

Then the wastes pass to the bladder and then to the urethra. About 150 liters (33 gallons) of fluids pass through your **kidneys** every day. Ninety-nine percent of this is cleaned and goes back to your blood.

What is the skeletal and muscular system?

It enables the body to move. The bones and the muscles that are attached to them, with all the joints and ligaments, let you move your body parts such as arms and legs, bend your body, look to your right side or left side by moving your neck, and do the many other movements your body can do.

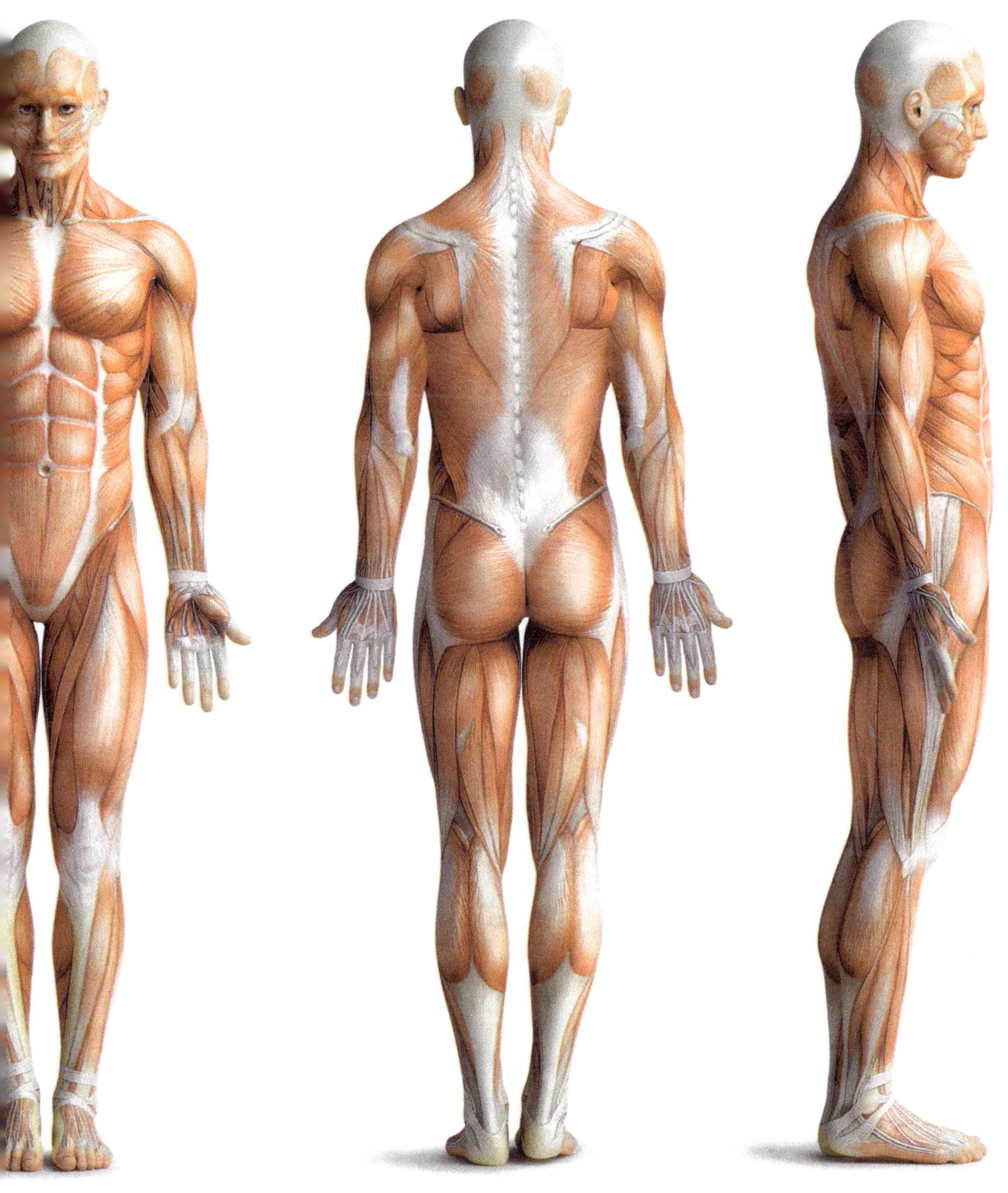

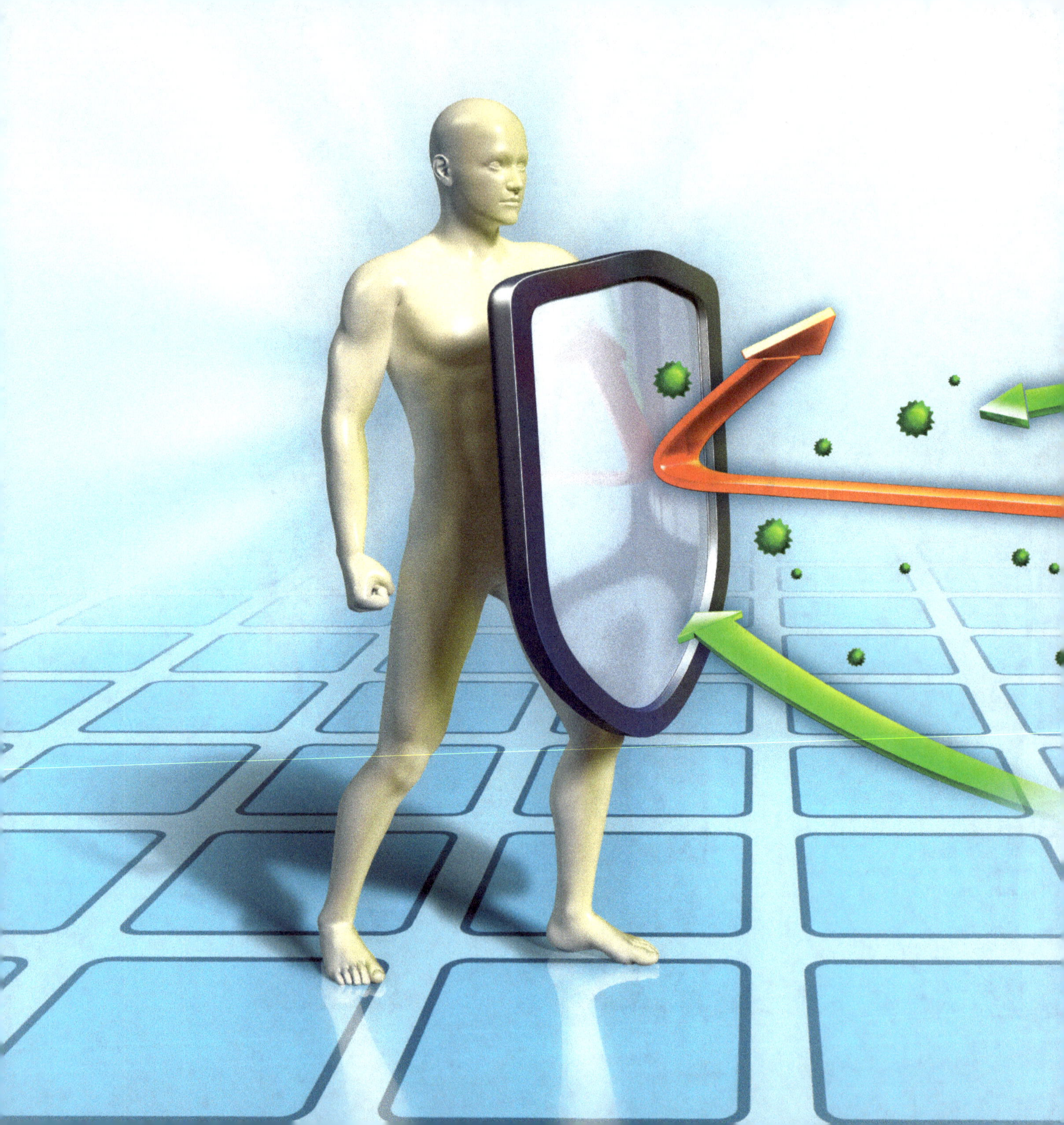

What is the immune system?

This is the body's defense against disease-causing bacteria and viruses.

What is the reproductive system?

This is responsible for the production of offspring. How this works depends on if you are a boy or a girl.

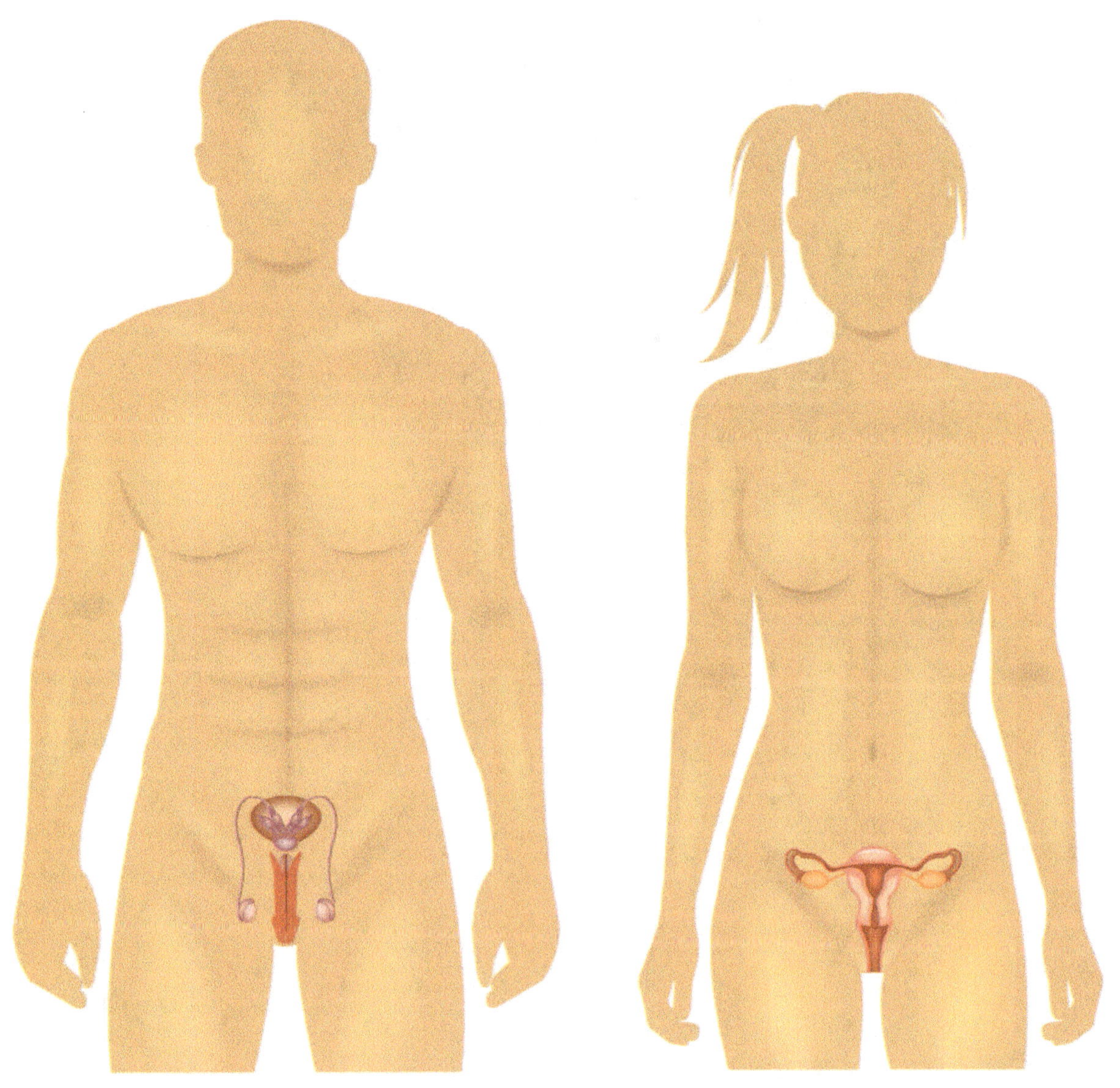

Male and female reproductive system

Now that you know the body parts and how they function, you can help it work well by eating healthy food.

Take care of your body so all of its parts function and help you live a happy life.

HEALTHY LIFESTYLE

YOURSELF ...AT YOUR BEST!

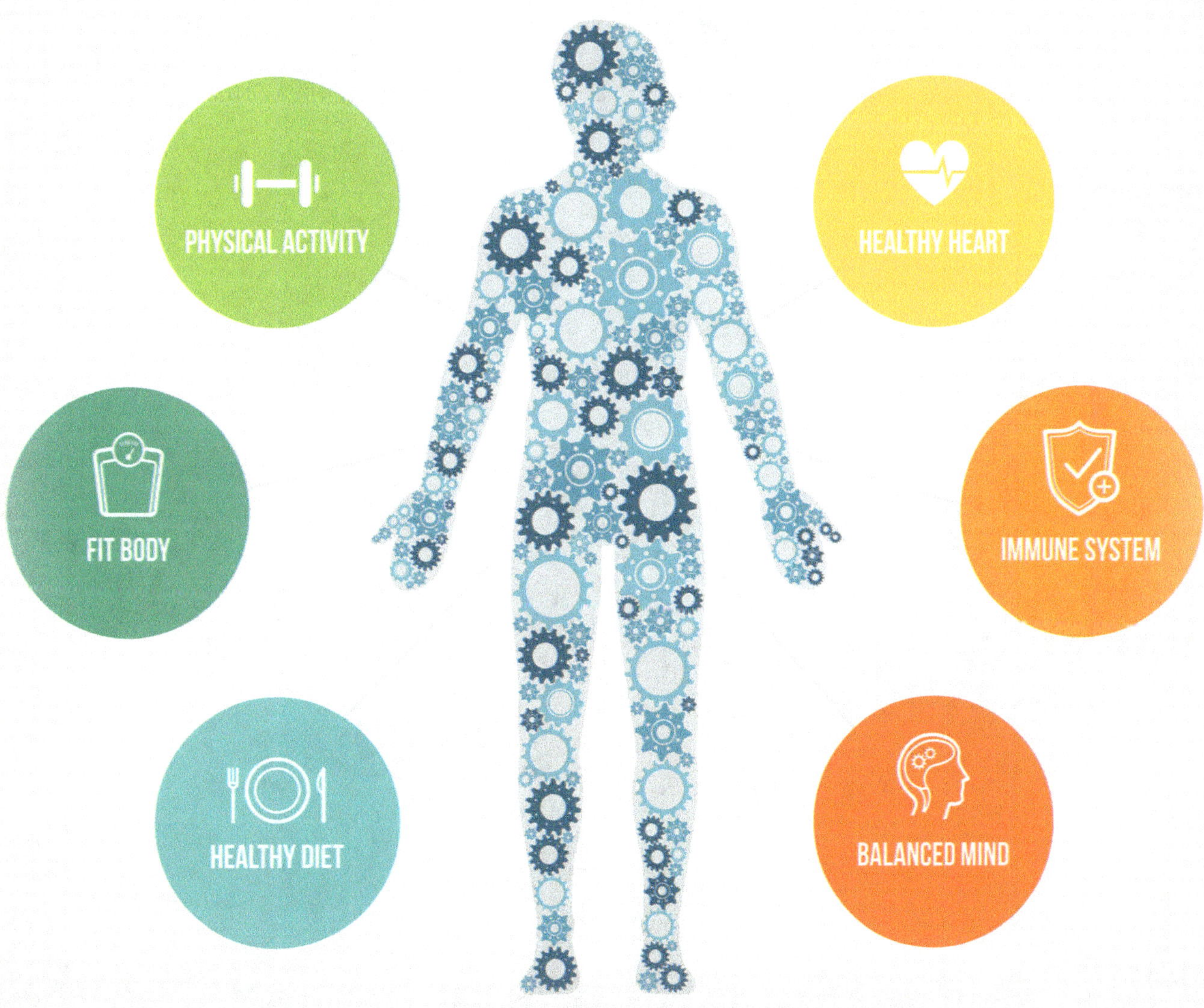

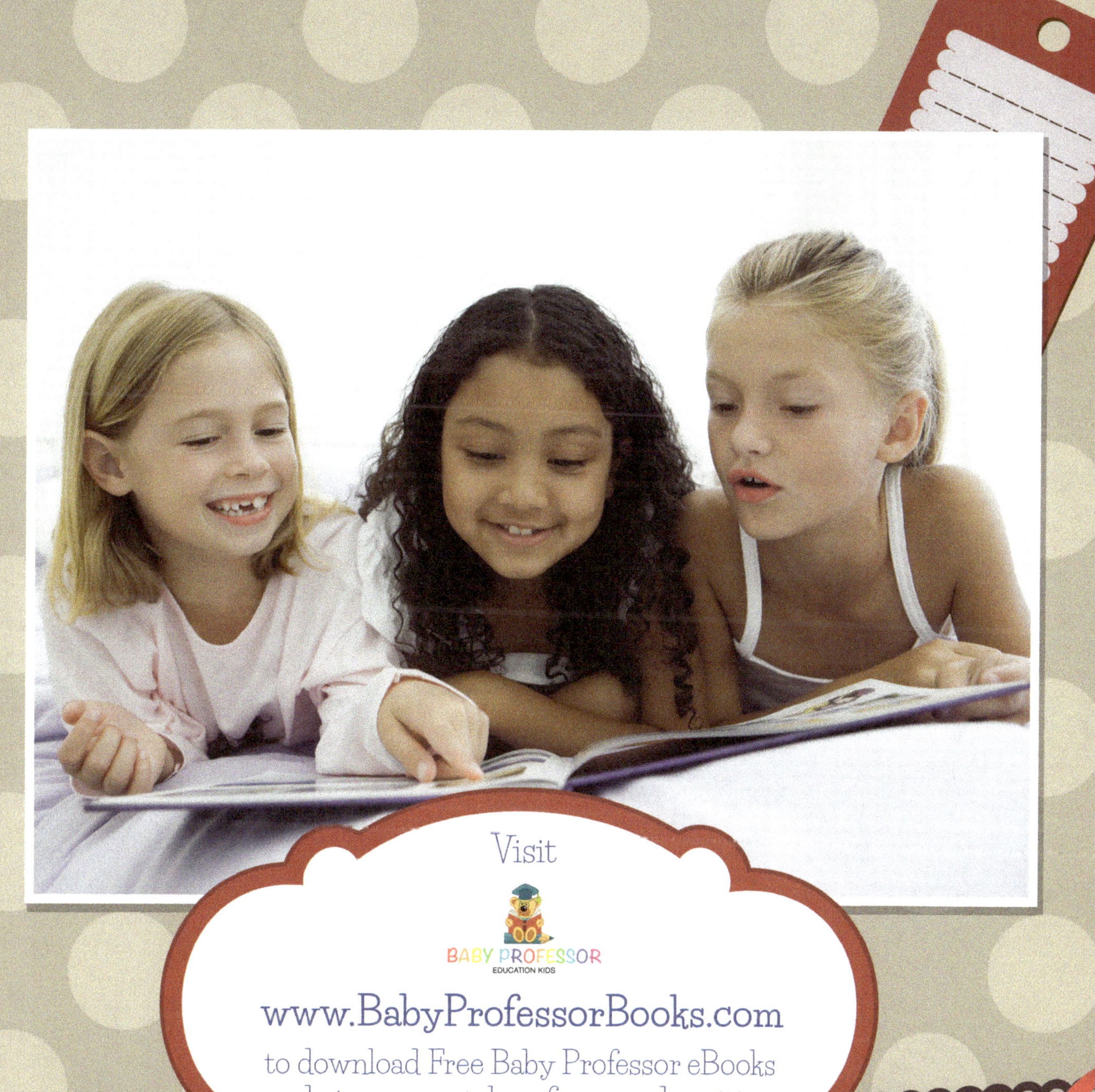

Visit

BABY PROFESSOR
EDUCATION KIDS

www.BabyProfessorBooks.com
to download Free Baby Professor eBooks
and view our catalog of new and exciting
Children's Books

www.ingramcontent.com/pod-product-compliance
Lightning Source LLC
LaVergne TN
LVHW082302150826
845677LV00009B/1702

* 9 7 9 8 8 6 9 4 4 2 7 5 8 *